Pleuvoir

by Anjee

National Library of Canada Cataloguing in Publication Data

A cataloguing record for this book that includes the U.S. Library of Congress Classification number, the Library of Congress Call number and the Dewey Decimal cataloguing code is available from the National Library of Canada. The complete cataloguing record can be obtained from the National Library's online database at: www.nlc-bnc.ca/amicus/index-e.html

ISBN 1-4120-2556-7

TRAFFORD

This book was published *on-demand* in cooperation with Trafford Publishing. On-demand publishing is a unique process and service of making a book available for retail sale to the public taking advantage of on-demand manufacturing and Internet marketing. **On-demand publishing** includes promotions, retail sales, manufacturing, order fulfilment, accounting and collecting royalties on behalf of the author.

Suite 6E, 2333 Government St., Victoria, B.C. V8T 4P4, CANADA

Phone	250-383-6864	Toll-free	1-888-232-4444 (Canada & US)
Fax	250-383-6804	E-mail	sales@trafford.com
Web site	www.trafford.com	TRAFFORD PUBLISHING IS A DIVISION OF TRAFFORD HOLDINGS LTD.	

Trafford Catalogue #04-0384 www.trafford.com/robots/04-0384.html

10 9 8 7 6 5 4 3 2 1

The fight rages on-
It is weak to succumb

1

If I had wings,
Would I fly away
Or clip them
And stay...

2

Breathing down my back
Voices filling up my head
Eyes fogging over
Heart's convulsing
Can't catch my breath
Can't get a grip
The devils laid hands

Have a feeling
Need to be somewhere
Not of this place
Far away from here
Got off the wrong exit
Miles away from home
Lost

3

Out of the light
The darkness creeps
Swirling blackness
Hovering, always near
Stumbling and falling
Drenched in my disease
Wasted in this
Try to run away
Hands grabbing me back to stay
Wants to feed
Can never get enough
Not strong enough for you
Didn't listen
Now I'm lost
Surrender to this hole
Life of discontent
Failure all around
Sweet smell of deceit
Distorted happiness
A memory of a dream
Nailed shut
Tortured for past sins
Awash in blood
To remind me
Broken and cold
To break me

The memory of you
To kill me

4

The lowliest meaning
I must keep to myself
Can never shed a tear
Can never tell the truth
Must make you believe
All is well with the earth
I must lie with disgrace
Lie right to you face
You can never know the secret
That pounds within my chest
Never know the sorrow
Never know the pain
Never know the loneliness
That eats me away
I bleed with every breath
Though you can not
See the wounds
I will not let you see
Deep within myself
That door has been closed
The key has long been lost
The walls are built with steel
Nobody is ever going to get across
Although I seem to be
Laughing ecstatically
The pain is ever growing

And is binding intensely
Leave me to survive
In my lunatics dream
Where the monsters are real
And the darkness never retreats

5

Wandering down the road I made
Wondering about the choices
That have led me here
Living blind to the light
Breathing in the fog
Clouding my dreams
Gave up on my life
But the blood still pumps
The heat still flickers
I've got to get out
But the weak won't listen
I keep walking
I'm searching to believe
If I still have hope
I will find the meaning

6

I am nothing
Just a bit of cold air
Nothing at which to stare
A hollowed out shell
A lump of skin
I don't care
A blackened room
Something to match my mood
No energy No light
Nothing left to fight
Don't like me
Don't like you
Just leave me here
No feeling No life
All my dreams destroyed
In the light
Nothing is left
Don't pretend to ask
I am nothing
I am lost
I am the moon
I am the sun
I am the night

7

I'm dying and nobody sees
I'm falling apart and nobody sees
I'm broken and nobody sees
Am I the only one with sight
How do you not see the disease
Festering and cracking
How can you not see

I can kill with a glance
I am death and it is me
I was picked for this
The dark man in my head
Whispers my demise

The world is blind
Wake up and see
Open your eyes
See what I see
The waste and the filth
Crawling all around me
Look and see what your world
Has done to me

I can kill with a glance
I am death and it is me
I was picked for this

The dark man in my head
Whispers my demise

How did it come to this

8

Enter my insanity
Trying to break free
Always running into walls
Always trying to ruin me
Taking away my life
My reason for existence
They're breaking me
Sucking the energy away
Can't make them stop
The well is nearly dry
Don't have much left to give
My light barely glimmers
A cold wind runs through me
Wasted and tired
My dreams make me cry
Death my greatest friend
See through my eyes
Live through my pain
You'll never know
You never will
You can't have me
No one ever will

9

Deeper and deeper
I'm falling, descending
Through the stormy sky
Don't know where
I lost everything
It hurts to cry
Don't think I'll ever get back
To where things are right
It's gone
Cold runs in me
I'm old, stale
Everything slips
Through my wrinkled hands
Nothing works anymore
Wind rushes past
Don't want to think
The pain is overwhelming
The only thing that I feel
The one thing that thrives
My heart bleeds out
An open angry wound
For all to see
I can only remember
All the wrong
If only I knew
The right words

To let it all go
Falling faster
No way to stop this flight
Descending into the black
Nothing before me
Nothing behind
Just a life wasted
A useless nothing
Time holds no meaning
I lost it all
I just want to go home
But I never know
Where it was
Just sat by
Bringing my nightmares alive
Let them eat me up
I'm dissolving in the mess
The mess I made
Never happy here
Just a crazy notion
I made myself believe
How could it come to this
All the dreams in my head
I've never believed in myself
So it's come to this
Falling, falling, falling
To my death
Look into my dead eyes
I once was alive

If only for a moment
Now the fear has taken over
I've lost the will to fight
It's killing time
And I am the one casualty
I pray for it to end
So I can live once again
Pray for the rain
To make me whole again
Kiss me goodbye
And walk away
I don't want you to see
My broken body on the ground
All alone
But with a smile on my face
It's finally over

10

I heard a lonely cry
From beyond
Barely a whisper
I heard my name
Over and over
Calling to me
I ran to where
I thought it would be
Over the cliff
And into the sea
Pulling me
Further and further
Until it enveloped me
Carrying me into his arms
He buried me
Deep into the sea
To be with him always
Moaning
He loved me
Yes, now I believe

11

The worst dream
All alone in the dark
No one you see
Frightened and old
The realization
It's not a dream
Your nightmare
Is alive
The kiss of death
Whispers your name
Sad eyes
Looking back at you
Helpless
Want to sleep
But the dark
Grabs you back again

12

Weariness persists
Eating away
Falling again
Too tired to stop
How black is the view
Skin falling off bone
Can't seem to make it stay
Secrets whisper
A voice I no longer know
The world passed on by
Didn't even see it go

13

Exquisite corpses
Covered in dried blood and grime
Naked with sweetest decay
Take me with you
Whispers in the dark
Dead empty promises
Desperation cries
Melting my withdrawal
Piles of bodies
Rotten to the core
A thousand lives
Try to pull me under
The punishment of life
So hard for me
The perfume of death
So heavy with stench
I'd love to lie with them
Covering me with their disease
To die in their arms
The beautiful songs they sing
Puts me to sleep
To dream of the end
The one thing I live for
I'm afraid that they will win

14

Break everything I touch
Everything that matters so much
A fire burning, blazing so high
If you get too close
You'll burn to the bone
Your burning flesh will fall away

Cover up the angry hole
Ugliness seeping through
This costume of sanity
Is not working anymore

Labyrinth of confusion
Hide myself from view
This hurt is all I have left
Charred to the core
A masterpiece of destruction
A lifetime in the making
Won't have it any other way

15

Somewhere in the dark
I feel your presence
Guiding me through
A hand on my shoulder
Whispering in my ear
A shadow of dreams
I'm not quite sure I've had
A distant pull
Of a ghostly place
This heaven of hell
You are always near
The darkness is vast
The waves crash upon the shore
Filling my lungs
Dragging me down
Sending me to the cold
Sinking
Waiting
To be released
If only for you
Together in death
We've found home

16

I've carried this aching
For as long as I have known
I look up at the sky
Watching my courage
Pass me by
Stuck in this life
I don't want to be
Can't find a reason why
When am I to be
This loathing and disgust
Keeps tearing me down
I scream and I scream
But no sound ever comes out
I keep you guessing
And my charade
Is almost a reality
Nothing is what I believe
My life is useless to me

17

I awake everyday
Hoping that today
Will be the day
It all ends
All the sadness
All the pain
My black dead heart
Barely beats
It's almost the end
I want all of this
To go away
I'm almost finished
My life has stopped
I've reached the point
I can let it all slip away
I hurt too much
To begin again
I can't afford to see the light
The sun stopped shining long ago
The cold is in my soul
The tears no longer flow
I am numb to it all
I can't carry on anymore
My blood will run
Until my very last breath
Then my poor heart

Can give up the fight
I will finally be gone
And I will never come back

18

If you prick me
I do not bleed
If you hit me
I do not feel the sting
If you set me aflame
I do not feel the heat
I live in a black and white world
I cannot feel a thing
And yet I can see you watching me
Hate flows from your eyes
Trying to destroy me
I do not care
You can do nothing to me
My walls are strong
You can't even come close
I sit in the center
All alone in thought
Frozen in time
Nothing gets in
Nothing gets out
So you do what you want
You don't even exist
In my empty space
My ice cold world
My lonely place
The only one

Alone
I can't get out

19

How will I ever feel like I belong
When I have never felt before
Boiled and tarred
Hung out for the eyes to see
A place for the spit to hang
My eyes see nothing
Only concentrating on the black within
Finding a place of horror and intrigue
Come feel my twisted release
See if you can stay alive
All the others left me
Your pain helps my dead inside
To see you struggle under me
I see a spark of life in these veins
Of only death and torture
Is how I can manage to survive
In your suffocating perfect world
I sit back and laugh
You think you have me
But it is I who has you
I am the reflection
You wish not to see
I am the demon in your soul
Your downfall
Your destruction
Your death

You need me

20

Razor wire holding
Wrapped tighter still
Beating too hard
Locked up tight
A few have tried
Nobody gets inside
They think they know
Run screaming again
To catch a glimpse
It doesn't matter
It's never attempted twice
Laugh as you run and hide
After all this life
Can't blame me for
Looking to death
It's torture to stay alive
Everything inside is gone
Just a hollow shell
Filled with nightmares
Grotesque and bleeding
Wouldn't want to stay
Can't blame you for
Treating me this way
I know

21

Wanted to do right
But I just did it wrong
Lunacy finds a way
It takes its stabs in the dark
What's been hidden
Is starting to show
Fighting back against
The big black hole
Scabs are falling away
Angry sores are flowing
Disease and decay
Are left exposed
Funny how nobody sees
The hurt on my face
The world keeps turning
Revolving around the pain
Where are you
All alone in my sin
Who will ever know
The kind of aching I feel
Sanity left me here
Mania taking it's toll
Things didn't turn out
The way it was supposed to
Here I lay
Living with my fear

Spinning out of control
This is what it feels like
Sinking, crying, cold

22

Silence a menacing sound
Swirling mass so thick
Cuts off thoughts
Glazed eyes blazing
Living but not realizing
Where it is I've been
Tried to fix myself
But just can't make it stick
Want to just belong
But nothing seems to fit
Seems like I fell
Can't see the ground
Wandered around
Into endless circles
Dizzy beyond words
Nothing to hold on to
I'm lost in the world
Nobody left to see
Burning before your eyes
Who would ever believe me

23

A kiss from heaven
That sears my soul
A gift for someone
Collapsing
In this fiery hole

24

Dead
Inside
Dead
Dark
Dead
Dropping
Dead
Foggy
Dead
Broken
Dead
Wasted
Dead
Used
Dead
Hungry
Dead
Fearful
Dead
Cold
Dead
Blind
Dead
Tired
Dead
Lost

Dead
Waiting
Dead
Wanting
Dead
Please...Dead

25

Beautiful sight to behold
From the darkness
Down below
Throbbing pain
With each crashing wave
Smell of deceit
On each passer by
Fill me with the sweet sounds
Destruction
Cutting and burning
Scar me for life
Revel in the bittersweet
The blackest night
The darkest pitch
There is no light
But one shining star
To guide me through
On my way to find you

26

The old and ancient
Shattered and bruised
I am this
Surrounded by innocence
Feeling dirty and uncleansed
Weeping sores
Covering me
Hiding in my filth
So no one can unearth
The richest part of me
Struggling to breathe
I want you to understand
But I can't find you
Blazing to hell
Silent screaming
Pounding in my chest
Beating in my brain
Wanting to love
But I am breaking
Slowly but surely
Death awaits me
But I'm fighting
I'm shining
I'm failing

27

I refused all that was given me
I didn't want to conform to your lies
I always kept myself on the outside
Didn't want to be like you
I made my own mistakes
Bitterness is on my side
All this pain I hide
I will never show it to you
I hide underneath this smile
I want to trick you
You can never know what lies beneath
Piles of memories
That I conveniently numbed over
I can't feel anything anymore
I couldn't even if I tried
It would take more than I could give
It's as dark as it can get
I'm watching everything revolve
As I sit here with my decay
The time seems to fly
And a second lasts forever
All at the same time

28

The pain like a star
Lighting up the sky
The cuts lay so deep
Only feel through
A heartbeat
Let the ground
Swallow me whole
The spirits invite
Me to stay
To be so weak
Is to give in
-You know-
They threw me out
The sea of humanity
The devils spawn
Take it away
They'll never understand
The battle is all upstream
Against all creation
Simmering in hatred
The war is about
To begin

29

Bound by hands and feet
Covered but left exposed
The world walks by
Pretending not to see
My insides slipping
Bloody and ripe
Falling at my feet
Soon there will be
Nothing here left of me
A black cloud hovers
Covers me in shame
My crown of thorns
Weaves a web of agony
Coursing through my soul
The loneliness threatening
Forever descending
A deep black hole
I'm collapsing

30

The voices inside my head
Drive me to harm
It takes everything inside
To push them away
I fight the good fight
Just to keep my defenses up
I just wish there was someone
To help me keep my head
Up off the ground

31

Despair and loneliness
Eat me alive
It seeps out my pores
Covering me in grime
Wondering if my memories are just a mistake
Buried everything for so long
Can't remember right from wrong
Can you feel this old
And not have lived
Can you look inside
And tell me what's wrong
I haven't ran
I haven't tried
I'm planted firmly down
My roots prevent me to fly
The undesired all this time

32

I'm afraid of what's inside
A dark place of secrets and rage
Bubbling with time
Insisting to boil over
If I give it half a chance
It will take me over
So let down your guard
So this hate can begin
The anger is seething
Rolling at a fever pitch
Threatening to erupt
Accept the evil within
The fight is wearing thin
Don't want this part of me
Look into my eyes and feel the anguish
It's eating me insane
Listen to it growing stronger
Watch me rot from the inside out

33

Swirling masses of emptiness
Black clouds hover overhead
Raining misery in torrents
Drenching my very soul
Hot tears of torment
Sliding down my face
Blinding winds pushing me down
Chilling to the bone
Wandering alone in need
No eyes to see
No arms to hold
No heart to feel
Doubt stabs painfully
As death beckons beautifully
The only light I see
I will follow through
To find the peace I seek
I will find you

34

Beyond the light
So much sorrow
So much death
Cold hands grip my skin
Breathless and screaming
Crouching in fear
Living the night
A fire burns bright
Can't get anywhere near
Nightmares fade in and out
My life flashes before me
Naked and scared
Bones of mistakes
Flung at my feet
Furious pounding
Foaming with lunacy
See the madness within
Insane from the start
Decisions not made
Tear me apart
Shamelessly believing
I am not a part
Life has no meaning

35

Lunacy chasing
Down corridors
Misplaced my plan
Flee to paralyze
Deaden the mind
Drawing closer
Skeletal hands
Grasping air
Almost catching
Hyperventilating
Hot and sweaty
Heart pounds
Deeply petrified
Dreams of madness
Soul wanting
Psychopathic
Trying to win
Blindly running
Again

36

Undue torture
Rains on my soul
Can’t see out
Blackness seeping in
Death is the answer
Death is the key
It just might save me

37

Behind the bloody garden pole
Water smells up deaths drive
Repulsive, drooling, screaming
She cried

38

You must boil our death crush
The moaning void eternity recalls
Smearing rain as shadows
Frantic, shaking, weak, and raw
Through a beauty's black stare
Still a bitter sordid dream

39

Knifed the languid tongue of men
I whisper heaving blood
Manipulate my ornate sin
Trudge there by sleep
Bare and like water
Vison insane gift

40

Torrents of red cover my skin
The slash of my throat opened wide
Letting light and warmth filter in
The poison slithers out
Searching for a new host to attack
Death comes for me
To set me free and take me home
Peace at last

41

Dirt caked under these nails
Full of filth and gore
Tried to scrub it clean
Won't go away
No matter how hard I try
It always stays
Can't get clean
Bloody and raw
Can't go back
To how it was before
I try so hard
It isn't enough
Scream so loud
But it's all gone
Try to fight
It's too hard
Want to go back
I've lost the touch
Knife in my back
Paralyzed with pain
Tried to live
Don't know how
Where is all the light
It's all black
Take it all back
I don't want this anymore

42

Hey you
You with your worthless dreams
Hey you
You with your worthless life
Hey you
I'll give you something you want
I'll give you some meaning
I'll give you someone to follow
Hey you
Show me your fake smile
Hey you
Show me your empty head
Hey you
Show me you hollow heart
Follow me down
Follow me down
Follow me down to here
I'll show you the way
Show you the way to insanity
You'll wish you'd never met me
I'll rip you apart
I'll leave you begging for more
Hey you
Follow me down
Follow me down
Follow me down to here

Welcome to your worst dream come true
You'll learn to love me
You'll learn to love this
Hey you
Follow me down
Follow me down
Follow me down to here
Hey you
I'm lying in wait
Hey you
You'd better watch out
Hey you
I'll get you before long
Hey you

43

Leave me alone
I can't feel
Don't want to be me
Full of total darkness
And despair
I'm too bitter
To consume
Burning in hell
Right here on earth
Flashes of pain
Coursing through
Take me by surprise
What am I to do
Don't come near me
I will hurt you
I've locked myself up
It's for my own good
My evil is put away
It's safer for you
I can't be let out
Keep the monster in
And it all fades away

44

Pathetic little girl
Silly dancing fool
Lying sack of shit
Destroys you with a touch
Don't get too close
Her fire burns too hot
She'll devour your soul
Rip you to shreds
Dangerous tiny thing
Watch her eyes glow
The spell she weaves
The secrets she knows
Your mind she wants
She'll suck you dry
And leave nothing behind
Evil thing she is
She'll make you want to die

45

Beyond the twilight sky
Lonesome cries discontented
Wanton needs crucify
Mortal thoughts tormenting
Stamp out the light
Wherefore blackness lies
He shall be
Seeking out his lady true
Wicked loathing seemly curse
Hunting herein and there
Perilous to foulest death
He will find her
Hanging by a lonely thread
One foot into the abyss
Together makes one
They will fly
Hearts together bound
Two lovers unite
Sanctified

46

Always under my chain
Ache worshiping the blows
Power beneath the screams

47

I see myself drowning
In a pool of death and decay
The flies already are hovering
Waiting to lay their eggs in my skin
They will bring new life to these bones
But I won't be living
With my spirit broken through time
It's just so easy to give in
What loneliness can do
The pain bursts right through
It had no where else to go
You can only bury so much
Before you overflow
I'm done waiting for my time to come
I think it passed me by
Didn't see me sitting so still
I'm a wasted mess
Waiting to be swept away
Forgotten and unfulfilled
Just some useless space

48

Showers of neglect and boredom
Rain down on my head
Drenching me cold
I am scared
Fears of myself falling
Driving towards madness
Shaking and in tears
The void lays before my eyes
So black and consuming
Waiting to pull me in
Empty thoughts hold me back
Wanting to jump in
Is this the answer to my prayers
I want to give in
Desperation clouds my desires
The blood is so warm when I bleed
Deaths beauty is hypnotizing
Is this all but a dream
I awake deaf and screaming
All of this in my head
I continue living

49

Take the shadows sweat
Recall raw blue chanting
Frantic panting falling screaming
Repulsive picture of madness
A storm my love
May shake me like death

50

December has arrived
Thinking backwards about May
The world at my feet
And how I pissed it away
Thinking about what could have been
And what I could've done
December has come
Too old now to dream
My time is almost gone
And if I could relive my life
I wouldn't do this again
I'd find a way
To undo all the wrong
In a different place
In a different time
I'm ashamed of what I've become

51

I want to go below
Down to the ocean floor
Breathing in the water
Drowning
I want to take you there
Come with me
Live with me
Taste the fear
It's calling me
Make it hurt
I want to feel the need
Feel the pain
Love me here
We are one and the same
I won't ever go away

52

I want to remove myself from life
Take myself away from here
From the black cloud over my head
To the shadows that follow
Whisper away the fear
Away from the likes of you

53

A thousand whispers
In my head
Storming repulsiveness
Weak behind you
Screaming delirious dreams
A black bitter stare
Driving me mad

54

Waiting
In someone else's life
Waiting
Near collapse and delusion
Waiting
In exasperation and exhaustion
Waiting
For the door to be opened
Waiting
On my knees in humiliation
Waiting
For the hysteria to take over
Waiting
The clock is ticking
Waiting
With rage and regret
Waiting
In shame and servitude
Waiting
For the torment to turn to triumph
Waiting
For you to appear
Waiting

55

Trying to find a reason
Can't contain the rage and hate
Feel so old and rotten
Could break apart if you pushed
Want to find a way out of here
My nightmares are my pleasure
My life is the hell in which I dwell
So cold a blizzard rages inside
Icicles forming in my brain
I'm slowly shutting down
Watch me fade away from here
The dark lives with me always
Don't care to see the light
Always failed me when I needed it
Ascending into nothingness
Don't try to help unless you want a fight
Can't remember if I want anything else
Maybe I like living in the gloom
Maybe it's the only way I know how

56

This pain in my brain
Reminds me again and again
Of what I remember from way back then
It brings me down here
To a black place of thorns
Reminds me of the razors slice of sweetness
I left behind a lifetime ago
I condemn myself to live like this
With the mistakes I made
To try not to repeat them
I can't even look myself in the eyes
I see the worthless trying to live
A disgusting heap of decomposing flesh
Sinking down in silence to my own private hell
Lingering on, gasping for life breath
Until the filth I've flung
Will engulf in an explosion of flames
And reduce me to nothing but ash
Then blow me out of your way
And pretend I never existed

57

So much time to dream
So much time to live
So many decisions to make
So many disappointments to have
So many people shove you
So many disapproving looks
So many words thrown
So many tears shed
So many times your heart bleeds
So many thorns in your side
So many screams held inside
So many things that erupt
So many fists thrown at the sun
So many questions why
So much love to give
So much it hurts inside
Don’t know what went wrong
I never asked for this

58

Dark thoughts dreaming me awake
Warmth sliding
Deliciously slow
From the cuts I know that aren't there
Must fight the desire
But the voices scream louder
The pleasure amplifies
Run faster
Wake up from the thirst
That pulls me deeper
Can never give in
Will not give them the satisfaction

59

Discover evil ground
Prisoner of dark fire
Drink life blood
Together for eternity

60

Endless empty
Unfillable abyss
Dragging pushing
Kicking screaming
Crushing meaningless
Blowing apart
It hurts to breath
I do not belong

61

Swept away
Down a winding path
Breathless and cold
Waiting for eternity's call
Black and blue
Crying uncontrollable
Mind is numb
To it all
Can't conceive
How I lived this long
No fascination in life
Nightmares
In every heartbeat
Your lips form lies
Hiding behind the disguise
Old withering
Complicated goodbyes

62

The destroying force
That paralyzes
Soaked to the bones
A tsunami of pain
Crashing upon
Your already broken back
Misery filling your lungs
Your breath explodes
Chains of desperation
Weigh you down
Falling through depths
Deeper and darker
Bubbling screams
Thrashing limbs
Your heart breaks
Sinking faster
Your life flashes
No more fight
Water swallows

I am released

63

Screaming night
Moonlit dream
Lost innocent
Shatters serene
Tattered bare
Struggles graze
Unintelligible shriek
Cast unfound
Quietly undone
Afflicted abound

64

The tears that
Threaten to flow
Disguised in a smile
My heart beats sickness
My heart bleeds pain
Just when I figure it out
Something always
Breaks me down
A never-ending journey
Of torment and fear
A lifetime of hell
A solemn promise
Of evil and dread
Conflict and rage
Crawl beneath my skin
Searching blindly
Towards the light
All alone
Tired of the waste
Stumbling in the gloom
Repulsive shadowy taste

65

Screaming alone weak
Bitter sleep under rain
Sad ache beating red
Picture black poison
Leave the beating light
Cry a thousand lies
Dreams filled with death
Blinding my eyes

66

The denial
The lies
The high
The low
The deception
The weary
The neglect
The rejection
The pathetic
The wicked
The weak
The strong
The right
The wrong
The sick
The well
The hunger
The pain
The war
The storm
The snow
The rain
The cold
The ice
The beginning
The end

The light
The dark

67

The smell of the rot
Alive in the air
Opening it's arms
To welcome you
The heat hovers
While the ripe swells
The animals are ready to feast
A heavy pressure swarms
A weight crushes your heart
Your breath starts to pant
Flashes of life
Dancing through the light
The pain washing it away
Your body disintegrates
Raw rotting meat
Decaying feast for the afterlife
A humid rain
A fitting end
One lonely life

68

All alone
Except for the view
My desolate eyes
See instantly
The ravaged sin
Everyone's curse
Seeing the bitterness
On everyone's lips
Spewing foulness
On everyone living
I see anguish
The bloodless skin
Sickly and weak
Falsely deceiving
I see through this
Latched to my moldy perch
Except for the view
I am all alone

69

A man
Alone in dreams
Sheltered from view
Hiding from thoughts
Falling into other worlds
Running past shadows
Screaming eyes closed
Monsters eating red
Blinded with pain
Hiding away immobilized
Frozen in fear
Nothing inside

Death wings
Warms up the cold
With their death dreams
Fluttering in your head
Whispering like screams
Filling up the dark
Mouth is bound
Eyes nailed open
Their wings show you
Everything you thought
That couldn't be real
Shadows swirling
The darkness weeps
The walls bleed
Your skin flayed
Your sin revealed
Death wings
Fly through your soul
Taking your will to live
Taking your life
Feel the slicing of the knife

71

The ocean calls
Waves crashing
Water ice cold
Mesmerizing
Wave after wave
Stirring grieving
Distressing resentful
You feel the call
Unearthly and wise
Pulling you in
Black darkness
Guiding your way
Into the final light
Gratified

72

The devil has been calling
Can't seem to pull away
He gives me things so I want to stay
Makes it hard to run
Can't tell right from wrong
I really want to be good
But it's really hard
I'll start doing what he says
So I guess I'll stay in hell

73

The pain inside
Always intensifying
Almost paralyzing
But I feel nothing
Smothered by fog
Never a clear day
Living but not really
Can't find a way out
I try to escape
Sometimes see the sun
But the clouds roll in
And the pain kicks in
And the nothing takes over
Don't know how I got here
I'll probably never leave
Apparently paying for past lives
Paying for my sins

74

Scared lost
Been waiting
For what seems like forever
Can't seem to break through
Been losing my mind
Trying to find
Where emptiness lies
Buried alive
Horrors in my dreams
Ghost of the past
Chained to my mind
Heart splits a million times
Reliving all the wrong
Soul is shattered
What I am
Is a lie

75

As the body fell
The blood has stained
Sprayed along the wall
Puddles filling the floor
Swallowing up the cracks
With gore filled screams
Slithering cold death

76

Fighting against
The traps of senility
Trapped alone
Looking for a reason
To stay in this hole
Weary wasted infectious
Paralyzed in agony
Afraid of the sane
Beaten down despondent
Spiritless uninterested weak
Sick and delirious
Crippled with disease
Waiting for the end
Promises left only for the dead

77

Shadow dreams
Spider weavers
The darkness reigns
Lost eternally
In its murky depths
A prisoner captured
Endless silent screams
The broken wandering
Flailing in torture
Smells of blood death
Fading into the walls
Souls descending
The cold amplifies
The challenge too great
Forever destroyed
Forever too late

78

The barricades are locked
This monster machine
Clawing at my soul
Screaming in my brain
Killing me piece by piece
Wants my death
All quivering and red

79

Haunting inner dreams
Calling unto me
Twice by the sea
Once by the sky
Voices filling my ears
A warning flying by
Blood gushing by mouth
Endless burning fires
Children dying nearby
A razor acid rain
A dark black sky
Flowing rivers of gore
The remembrance of the dead
Death to us all
The keepers of the souls

80

The crowd of whispers
Voices bid me to run
Soaked in guilt
I force myself to stay
I can never be
As you all want it to
Keep myself buried
In the shadows I play
Try to keep from view
Don't want to fan the flames
All the rotten decay
I keep it close
That's what keeps me sane
Far away from prying eyes
I play it safe
Hiding form everyone
The tears drown out my soul
All alone in the world
Waiting for my time to fly

81

Raining through the sun
Drenching my skin
Washing away my everything
Drinking in the sky
Making it okay to live another day
Drowning in the storm
It sweeps me away
I let it envelop me
And carry me to another place
Where the memory of your face
Won't endlessly haunt my dying days

82

Prisoner of a thousand fates
The winters speak madness
Frozen in the flood of fire
Ice cold drops of hate
Drip continuously down my neck
Caught in a twenty year moment
Fear the corrupt forest
Lying to the moon
Watching the boiling sun
Blinded by radiant red
Falling beneath the curse

83

A shiny bright star
Blown away by mischance
My only light in the sky
Now left to fight it alone
I tried to remember the words
But my thoughts have long since stopped
My hearts stopped beating
I've wandered year after year
Trying to feel anything
The emptiness suffocates
My insides are nothing
Being blinded in the dark
Can't seem to lift my head
Too heavy to contemplate
Where is heaven
When you're burning in hell

84

When the shadows seem to move
Even though there is no one there
They seem to reach out
Wanting to jump inside
Feel their cold claws piercing
Ripping apart paper skin
Impaling amputating eliminating
Leaving you starving
Collapsing in the bloodshed
Crawl to your grave
And sleep in the tears
All bitter and withering
The end is now the beginning

85

Just want to watch others live
Don't want to get in their way
Running in a constant loop
Everyday the exact same
Repetition is game
No surprises no plans
I just watch you living your life
So I don't have to live mine

86

The scars of my solitude
Run deep and far
The clouds above my head
Darken my world
With a deathly cold
Wrapping my misery close
I keep on my lonesome journey
The blackness of night
Lights my way
The thundering rain
Warms my lifeless heart
All the things no one wants
Floods my emptiness of pain
I soak in the worthlessness
Feeding on what you refuse to feel
Bathing in your waste
Makes my hole complete
Years melt like snow
Troubles push me along
It all could be so lovely
If it wasn't so very wrong

87

The rain felt like tears
The moon was full and bright
It glistened off the knife in my hand
I've been feeling closed for awhile
But it's going to open up

It's going to open up wide
It's going to happen real soon
You see, I have this plan...